DISNEY PRESENTS A **PIXAR** FILM

THE INCREDIBLES
The Essential Guide

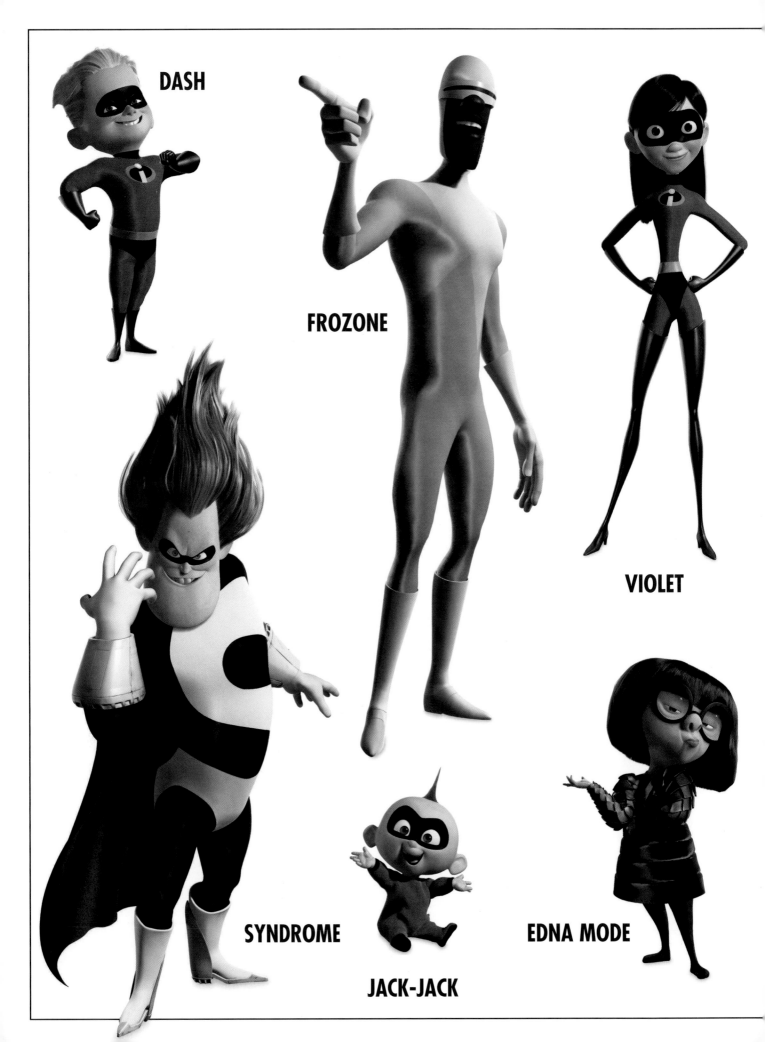

DASH

FROZONE

VIOLET

SYNDROME

JACK-JACK

EDNA MODE

DISNEP PRESENTS A PIXAR FILM

THE INCREDIBLES
The Essential Guide

ELASTIGIRL

MR. INCREDIBLE

Written by Stephen Cole

DK

CONTENTS

INTRODUCTION

There was once a time when heroes were admired members of society, protecting people from villainous plots and unfortunate accidents. However, in a surprising turn of events, citizens turned against the heroes, believing that they caused more trouble than good. They sued them for petty injuries, costing the government billions. The heroes were forced to retire and live their lives as ordinary people. But the world hadn't seen the last of the Supers, thanks to one quite *incredible* family....

MR. INCREDIBLE

In the golden age of Supers, there was one man who stood for all that was good and decent in the world… Mr. Incredible! This Super was everyone's favorite hero—until he found himself sued for saving someone who didn't want to be saved! Forced into hiding, Mr. Incredible hung up his suit. After fifteen years of living undercover, Mr. Incredible grows restless, until one day danger calls and he gets the chance to be Super again....

Golden days

In his heyday, Mr. Incredible's rugged good looks, easy charm, and, of course, his mega-strength made him the most popular Super by far. Loved by the public, many statues were made in his honor, and he received numerous awards.

Mr. Incredible is lured out of retirement by a computer message from a mysterious woman who offers him the chance to go on a top-secret mission. It doesn't take much to persuade him, and he's soon on a plane bound for the island of Nomanisan.

SUPER POWERS

- Mega-strength: strength level known to increase when in an intense emotional state.
- Near invulnerability: bodily impacts are ineffectual. May be harmed by energy beams and edged weapons.
- Uncanny crime sense: he can sense imminent danger.

Stylish new red suit made by Edna Mode, the world's top Super suit designer.

A six-ton tiki head comes in handy when Mr. Incredible needs to break through Syndrome's lava wall. Luckily, it isn't that heavy for Mr. Incredible!

SAVING THE DAY, ONE DAY AT A TIME.

Unknown to Mr. Incredible, his new Super suit has a built-in homing device. The new feature gives the exact location of the wearer at a touch of a button. Unfortunately, it goes off at just the wrong time!

Masked man

Every Super has a secret identity because, as Mr. Incredible says, "Who wants the pressure of being Super all the time?" To conceal his identity, Mr. Incredible wears a stylish black mask.

BOB PARR

Like many men, Bob blames his job and the stresses of family life for his hair loss.

Once the best-known, best-loved Super alive, Bob Parr is now fifteen years older and a whole lot heavier! Stuck in a job he hates, the former Mr. Incredible is limited to helping people with their insurance claims. Bob's frustrated by the predictable routine of family life and is always reminiscing about the past, but he soon realizes that his family is his greatest adventure.

Caught in the act

Bob has trouble controlling his mega-strength in public when he gets upset. After a miserable day at work, he drives home, only to slip on a skateboard, dent the car roof, and shatter the window! He lifts the car in frustration but puts it down when he sees a neighborhood boy watching!

With his modest salary from Insuricare, Bob buys his old Confinato as a sensible commuter car. Unfortunately, it doesn't offer much leg room, shoulder room, or head room for an ex-Super!

When Bob secretly resumes hero work, he earns triple his annual salary. He quickly ditches his old car for a sleek Mezza Vita sports car. Always the considerate husband, Bob also buys a new car for his wife.

New clothes reflect the new man.

Conference call

Bob knows that his wife, Helen, would be furious if she knew he was doing hero work again. He covers up his trip out of town by telling her that Insuricare is sending him to a conference. Helen is delighted the company is finally recognizing his talents.

Bob was late for his own wedding because he was out saving lives as Mr. Incredible! He married a fellow Super, Elastigirl, and the future seemed bright. But since they were ordered to retire from hero work, Bob finds it hard to adjust to "normal" family life.

Weigh to go!

When faced with the prospect of doing secret hero work on a regular basis, Bob realizes he has to get back in shape. He's put on a pound or two (or fifty!) over the years, so before he can fight crime once again, he has to combat his bulging waistline!

In training

If you're a Super, no "normal" gym will do. Bob goes to the local train yard, where he finds everything he needs to get himself back in top condition. He heaves huge tankers up and down, pulls freight trains along the track, and pumps iron with engines—a perfect workout for a Super who needs to shape up!

ELASTIGIRL

Cool, sassy, and independent, in her heyday Elastigirl was fast becoming one of the top Supers on the planet, with the power to stretch her body into any shape imaginable. Witty and competitive, she would often beat her future husband, Mr. Incredible, to the punch, insisting ladies go first! After heroes are banned, Elastigirl easily adjusts to family life, but when her husband goes missing, she's forced back into action and proves she's as Super as ever!

WHATEVER THE CRISIS, I'M FLEXIBLE.

Limber lady

In the golden age of Supers, Elastigirl was versatile, reliable, and a real go-getter! The young Super could never imagine herself living a "normal" life and wasn't interested in starting a family. But life for Elastigirl changed dramatically when Supers were forced to retire.

Jetsetter

When Elastigirl needs to get somewhere in a hurry, she can always call on her old friend Snug. If she needs a sleek and powerful jet, he can get her one in no time. Because of her advanced training, Elastigirl finds flying a plane after fifteen years as easy as riding a bike!

Elastigirl's new suit is made by Edna Mode, just like her husband's. This new suit, unlike her old flexweave suit, is virtually indestructible.

On the island of Nomanisan, Elastigirl must be quick-thinking and agile to enter Syndrome's secret base undetected.

High-kicking housewife

In her heyday, Elastigirl was famous for her ultra-powerful "stretched scissor-kick." It's fifteen years later, but Elastigirl's high kick is as awesome as ever—as Syndrome's guards soon find out!

Stretched to the limit!

When you can stretch your body through a villain's lair, you risk an unusual problem—getting parts of you stuck in closing doors! Even then, Elastigirl's not helpless, not by any *stretch* of the imagination! With her torso and legs caught, she still defeats five guards!

SUPER POWERS

- Super-elasticity! Elastigirl can bend, stretch, or twist her form into any shape.
- She can flatten herself as well as form a human parachute to slow someone's fall.
- Elastigirl can elongate her body, within a surprising limit, to become as long as she needs to be for the given situation.

HELEN PARR

Like most Supers, Elastigirl has a secret identity. Who wants to go to the grocery store dressed in a Super suit?! She is more commonly known as married mother-of-three Helen Parr. Unlike Bob, Helen has learned to put her Super-status behind her and focus on her family. She raises her kids with the same passion she once put into crimefighting and just wishes that Bob would do the same.

Wedded bliss?

On their wedding day, Helen and Bob swore to love each other no matter what happened. Their vows are put to the test when Supers are banned, and they're forced to live as civilians. Bob's desire to relive the past puts a real strain on the whole family—especially Helen.

When Bob is late home from bowling with his friend (and fellow Super) Lucius, Helen waits up for him. She spots a piece of rubble on Bob's shoulder and is horrified to discover that the pair didn't go bowling at all—in fact, they accidentally knocked down a building!

Helen's sensible pedal-pushers are stain-resistant—perfect for raising Jack-Jack.

Heroic housewife

Having Super powers takes the effort out of housework. Helen's amazing arms allow her to vacuum in every corner without moving an inch. She can pick things up from the floor without stooping, and if Bob's around, doing the chores is even easier!

Helen and Bob will always love each other. Violet is often embarrassed when her parents flirt with each other around the house!

The long arm of the law

When your kids have incredible Super powers, sometimes the only way to keep control is to use your own! When Dash and Violet fight, things can soon get out of hand—unless that hand is Super-stretchy and belongs to Helen Parr!

Helen becomes suspicious of her husband when she discovers his old Super suit has been mended. Bob only trusts one person with his suit, their old friend Edna Mode, so Helen calls her to find out what's going on.

VIOLET

GOTTA DISAPPEAR!

To the outside world, Violet is an ordinary teenage girl—shy, insecure, and with a crush on a boy who doesn't know she exists! But Violet is far from ordinary. Just like her parents, Helen and Bob, she's a Super. Violet has the amazing ability to disappear in seconds and can create force fields for protection. At first, Violet desperately wishes she were normal like everyone else, but eventually she learns that being a Super is in her blood.

Hidden powers

When Helen, Violet, and Dash are on a jet bound for Nomanisan and find missiles on their trail, Violet uncertainly tries to throw a force field around the plane. But the field is too small and weak, and Violet feels like she's failed. Helen reassures her that she has more power than she realizes—she just has to believe it!

Violet learns to create force fields around herself and float inside them for protection.

Helen leaves the children alone on Nomanisan while she looks for Bob, putting Violet in charge. The young Super is afraid— she knows the bad guys won't take pity on them just because they're kids. She practices her powers and slowly begins to gain confidence in herself.

For Super women, thigh-high boots are both practical and stylish!

Shrinking Violet

Violet is a very cool and clever kid—but she just doesn't believe in herself. She's so busy trying to be normal that she never gives herself a chance to shine. But when she's forced to fight with her family, that chance finally comes—and Violet gains the confidence she's always lacked.

Although Violet often wishes she were "normal," she sometimes finds that her powers come in handy—especially when Dash is teasing her about her crush on Tony Rydinger!

Clearly cool

When Violet turns invisible, *she* disappears but her clothes remain right where they are! But that all changes when Edna Mode creates a special suit for her that turns invisible whenever she does!

SUPER POWERS

• Violet can turn invisible at will. When she's wearing her Super suit, she becomes completely transparent!

• She can create powerful force fields. The force fields are strong enough to knock people flat, and they can even deflect bullets.

Double trouble

Stuck in the dense jungle on Nomanisan, Violet and Dash soon realize they must work together if they're going to survive. Violet's protective force fields and Dash's lightning-fast speed make the Super siblings more than a match for Syndrome's guards.

DASH

Dash's full name is Dashiell Robert Parr.

At just ten years of age, Dash is one of the fastest things on Earth. Competitive, a bit of a show-off, and full of restless energy, he often drives his family to distraction! Dash wishes he didn't have to keep his Super-speediness a secret—he's not even allowed to play sports at school in case anyone suspects his Super nature. Even though he knows it's against the rules, sometimes Dash can't resist using his powers in class to pull pranks on his least favorite teacher, Mr. Kropp!

When Dash is running at full-speed, he can outrun velocipods—Syndrome's island interceptors!

Dash looks like a sweet and innocent little boy, but he can be a little prankster at times!

Schoolboy schemer

Dash moves so fast that he's able to put thumbtacks on his teacher's chair in the middle of class without being spotted! Mr. Kropp suspects Dash is to blame, but he can't prove a thing. He tries to get evidence by setting up a video camera, but the "guilty little rat" is so fast, even the camera can't catch him in action!

Awesome appetite!

Dash has quite an appetite—not just for food, but for adventure! Like his dad, he feels Super powers are nothing to be ashamed of.

DASH IS MY NAME. SPEED IS MY GAME!

High-speed hits

Dash used to think all bad guys were like the ones on TV shows—but he soon discovers that real bad guys are a whole lot nastier. When face-to-face with one of Syndrome's guards, Dash makes up for his small size with lightning-fast punches!

With velocipods on his trail and a lagoon ahead of him, Dash fears he'll be caught. With few options left, Dash runs toward the water and is astonished to find he is so fast that he can run right across the water's surface!

On Nomanisan, Helen tells Violet and Dash to stay out of sight in a cave. But it's almost impossible to keep Dash still, and soon the little Super is off to explore. Unfortunately, he learns the cave they're in is actually the rocket exhaust tube from Syndrome's base!

SUPER POWERS

• Super speed—since he is a younger Super, the limits of his power have yet to be determined or fully developed.

• He can move so fast that not even a video camera can detect him!

• At top speeds, he can even run across water without sinking!

JACK-JACK

Little baby Jack-Jack Parr is the youngest member of the family and the odd one out! Jack-Jack is almost two years old, but the tiny toddler is showing no signs of having a Super power at all. He's good at doing what babies do best—dribbling, throwing food around at mealtimes, and talking gibberish, and that's about all! But there's still plenty of time for Super talents to emerge, and, if nothing else, Jack-Jack is incredibly cute!

Jack-Jack was born with auburn hair that never needs hair gel!

Even a baby needs to protect his secret identity!

Spoon it in, spit it out!

It's not a Super power as such, but Jack-Jack is an expert at dribbling his mashed-up baby food! As fast as Helen spoons it in, Jack-Jack can spit it out. Jack-Jack's favorite food is mashed carrots—his favorite game is to mash carrots!

Anything goes!

As far as Jack-Jack is concerned, the world is just one big playground. Whether he's being bathed by his mother in the kitchen sink or watching his older brother and sister quarrel, there's always a smile on his face! The only thing that really upsets him is if his family is truly distressed—then he starts crying like you wouldn't believe!

Daddy's boy

When Bob arrives home after a bad day at work, little Jack-Jack always cheers him up—he's the apple of his father's eye! Jack-Jack doesn't care that his dad used to be a Super. He loves his daddy no matter what!

SUPER POWERS

• Officially, his powers are unknown, but with his new red suit designed by Edna Mode, he sure looks like a little hero!

• He's excellent at throwing food during mealtimes.

• Not potty-trained.

Jack-Jack looks so sweet and innocent that his babysitter, Kari, thinks taking care of him will be a breeze. Little does she know that there's more to the toddler than meets the eye....

THE PARR FAMILY HOME

I t's taken three long years, but at last the Parrs are *officially* moved into their latest home after Helen unpacks the last box. The family has been forced to move more often than Helen would like because of Bob's inability to let go of the past. Each time Bob accidentally shows his Super strength, the Super Relocation Program uproots the whole family at great expense and relocates them somewhere new. Will this home last any longer than the others?

Mealtime mayhem

Life at the Parr house can be quite chaotic, with Violet and Dash fighting and Bob and Helen using Super powers to stop them! But even at home, they must be careful not to make the neighbors suspicious. If the doorbell rings, the family is always ready to resume "normal" behavior.

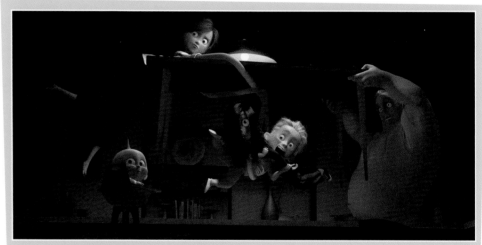

The garage is full of moving boxes and Bob's abandoned projects.

Like most of the houses in the neighborhood, the Parr house has very high windows— perfect for Supers who want privacy from their neighbors.

Family room

The Parr family room has been stylishly decorated by Helen to be good for the family and guests alike. Violet and Dash especially like the family room because they can easily slip in to eavesdrop on their parents' squabbles!

Something amazing

When Bob gets home from work, he often finds a kid called Rusty hanging out on the pavement. Rusty says he's just waiting around for something amazing to happen—and Bob knows exactly how he feels! Little do they know that the neighborhood's about to get a whole lot more exciting!

The Parr kitchen is a cook's dream with lime-green cabinets and a laminate counter. Helen makes a delicious chocolate cake that often gets devoured by Bob when he comes home late after a night of "bowling."

If there's one thing Bob enjoys about normal life, it's mowing the lawn. All of the neighbors are envious of his groomed front lawn.

As Mr. Incredible, Bob used to drive the Incredibile—a car with all the gadgets a Super could wish for. But now Bob needs an ordinary car to fit in with his ordinary life.

BOB'S DEN

Whenever Bob feels his dull life is getting the best of him, he retreats to his den. It's full of keepsakes and mementoes of the days when he was known and loved the world over as Mr. Incredible. He wishes he could turn back time, but all he can do is sit and stare at the fading memories lining his wall... that is, until he receives an unusual message offering him the chance to relive his glory days.

Mystery message

Bob finds a mysterious video screen in his briefcase that plays a message asking for the Super's help. Although hero work is illegal, Bob's soon on the phone accepting the mission!

Mr. Incredible was the poster boy for the Supers' public image campaign.

This was Mr. Incredible's first appearance on the cover of Life *magazine!*

A very grateful mayor gave Mr. Incredible the key to the city as a thank-you for his services.

A bronze statue created to honor Mr. Incredible as the world's top Super.

Secret mission

The message is from a woman called Mirage, who says she's from a top-secret government division. Bob takes notes as she outlines the mission: At a remote testing facility on the island of Nomanisan, a highly intelligent prototype robot is out of control and threatens to destroy millions of dollars' worth of research. It's up to Mr. Incredible to stop the unruly robot and save the day.

This valuable collector's item is the gun squashed by Mr. Incredible on his very first assignment.

The Super's record, "Mr. Incredible Sings," was so successful that it went quintuple platinum!

This was Mr. Incredible's 200th front-page story.

INSURICARE

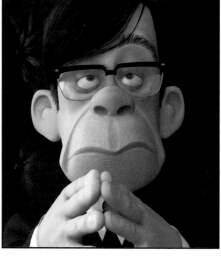

Saving the world, one insurance policy at a time—that's Bob Parr! Under the Super Relocation Program, Bob now spends his days working for Insuricare, possibly the worst insurance company in the world. The bosses of Insuricare are out to turn people's problems into profits for themselves! But Bob's still a Super at heart, and whenever he can, he secretly helps Insuricare's customers get the money they are owed.

Although the law requires that Insuricare helps its customers with their claims, Bob's boss, Gilbert Huph, seethes with rage each time a customer makes a successful claim. He only cares about Insuricare's stockholders; he'd turn down every claim if he could!

Each day, Bob sits in his painfully cramped office cubicle A113. Not wanting to arouse suspicion, he occasionally asks that his clients leave pretending to cry as he yells above the office walls, "I'd like to help, but there's nothing I can do."

Inside info

Mysteriously, Bob's neediest customers have an expert knowledge of how Insuricare operates—almost as if someone were helping them to penetrate the bureaucracy and find Insuricare's loopholes. Of course, Bob has no idea who this person might be....

Mrs. Hogenson is one of Bob's clients and another victim of Insuricare's heartless liability policy.

Bob's white shirt is size XXX Large, but it's still too tight!

From Huph's office window, Bob spots a suspicious character lurking in an alley.

Reprimand

Huph summons Bob to his office, determined to put a stop to Bob's caring attitude toward his customers! Halfway though Huph's lecture, Bob sees a man being mugged outside and is about to help him when Huph threatens to fire him.

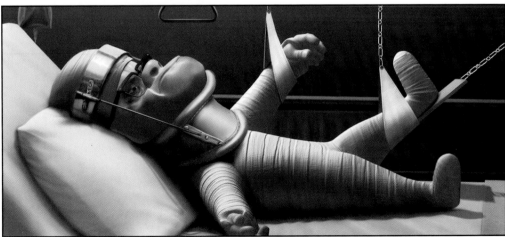

Don't push Parr too far!

Forced to ignore the mugger outside, Bob is finally fed up that no one will allow him to do great things anymore. Enraged by Huph's mean, uncaring attitude, Bob finally loses his cool. Huph pushes Bob too far and gets pushed right back—through four office walls, to be exact!

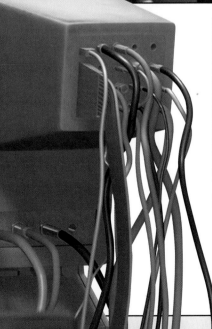

Fortunately, Huph survives, but it's up to Agent Rick Dicker from the Super Relocation Program to clear up Bob's mess. He has to keep the company quiet, pay damages, and erase the memories of all the stunned Insuricare staff who witnessed the incident!

Evasion countermeasures dispense caltrops, oil slicks, smoke pellets, rear-firing micro-missiles and velocity-suppressing goo.

Main solid propellant thruster

Ejector seat to remove unwelcome guests from car

Rocket turbine thrusters

High-tech instrument panel controls all the car's functions.

The radio in the Incredibile transforms into a high-tech tracking device. When there's a high-speed pursuit taking place, Mr. Incredible types "isolate pursuit" into a computer, and the vehicles involved appear on an aerial map of the city. In "merge pursuit" mode, the Incredibile will automatically follow the offending vehicle.

Intelligent tread allows tires to adjust traction to any surface at any speed. They are also puncture-proof, fireproof, and waterproof.

THE INCREDIBILE

Back in the days when Mr. Incredible was a Super, he had his own unique way of traveling in style… he would roar up in his Incredibile! Although he always worked alone, this car was the closest thing to a sidekick Mr. Incredible ever had. Highly automated, full of high-tech gadgets, cool, and comfortable, with a very reasonable rate of fuel consumption, it was the car every Super dreamed of driving.

En route to an emergency, Mr. Incredible can set the Incredibile to "autodrive" so he can take his hands off the wheel and change into his Super suit.

Windshield is bulletproof, fireproof, crushproof, bombproof, rocketproof, and tinted to reduce glare.

Emblem on hood glows.

SPECIFICATIONS

- Can be driven using a remote control located on Mr. Incredible's wristwatch.
- Classified as an MEV (multiple environmental vehicle).
- Has onboard weaponry.

Like Mr. Incredible, the Incredibile has a secret identity! At the touch of a button, the exterior transforms to look like an ordinary car.

Under the hood is not only a 2,000-pound thrust, 36-cylinder turbo compression atomic engine, but also an array of machine guns, micro-missiles, grappling cables, magnetic bombs, and torpedoes.

FROZONE

Anti-glare light refraction goggles.

Inline the age of the Supers, Frozone—Mr. Incredible's best friend—was the coolest hero around. With wit and style, and an amazing arsenal of freezing powers, Frozone was one cool customer. Now in retirement, he's just plain Lucius Best, and although he misses the good old Super days, he's learned, unlike Bob, to accept that they're long gone. In fact, Bob can sometimes be a bad influence, involving Lucius in illegal hero work that gets them both in trouble!

Thermal suit keeps body warm in sub-zero temperatures.

Freeze!

While saving innocent people from a burning building, Lucius and Bob find themselves accidentally breaking into a bank! The fact that they look like bank robbers in their ski-masks doesn't help when the police arrive!

Frozone can freeze people in their tracks without harming them—including this rookie policeman, who mistakes the pair for criminals. And before the law can thaw, they're gone!

KNOCKIN' VILLAINS OUT COLD!

SUPER POWERS

- Frozone has the power to generate ice from moisture in the air.
- He can freeze his opponents solid with an icy blast from his fingertips!
- Frozone is able to create his own transportation—ice skis, ice skates, and ice disks.

Ice disk: one option of Frozone's special boots.

Side by side

Lucius thought his heroic past would stay forever in cold storage…. But when danger looms and innocent lives are at risk, Frozone finds himself back in action alongside his old friend Mr. Incredible… after he finds out where his wife has put his Super suit.

Even as a civilian, Lucius is one super-cool guy!

In his day, Frozone was quite the ladies' man. Some say he was romantically linked to Blazestone. However, he settled down and now lives in a suave apartment in the city with his wife Honey.

Lucius was best man at Bob and Helen's wedding, and the whole family adores him. Each Wednesday, Bob and Lucius get together. Their wives think they go bowling—but they really hang out listening to the police radio and reliving their glory days.

EDNA MODE

Small in stature but big on style—that's Edna Mode, better known in Super circles as "E." Now a highly successful fashion designer, with exclusive collections modeled on catwalks all over the world, E was once the world's leading Super costume designer. She longs for the return of the Supers, so she can create suits that combine the latest technology with her own impeccable fashion sense!

Edna designs all her own stylish outfits.

Some of Edna's many Super suit designs.

E's clothes are made of the same high-tech fabrics and materials that she invents for Super suits.

Super designer

After Supers were banned, E's designs shifted from Supers to supermodels. Her work made her a wealthy woman, but nothing could compare to the thrill of designing for Supers. As far as E's concerned, there's nothing "super" about supermodels at all—they're spoiled, stupid little stick figures!

> ## THIS FALL, EVERYONE WILL BE WEARING BULLETPROOF.

Hall of fame

In a corridor that leads to her secret laboratory, E has an extensive collection of old Super costumes on display. They're all her own fabulous designs and remind her of the good old Super days!

When Bob's Super suit is torn during his secret mission on Nomanisan, he knows only one person qualified to repair it—E.

New suit

E examines Bob's out-of-date megamesh suit and is surprised that he's managed to damage the sturdy fabric. E guesses that Bob's moonlighting as a hero again, and she can't wait to make him a new suit. She decides it will be bold, dramatic, and heroic—and definitely *won't* have a cape!

Palatial pad

Edna's home is a stylish mix of the old and the new, filled with the latest modern technology. She commissioned the frieze on her back wall from a sculptor in Milan during last year's Fashion Week. Hidden gun turrets emerge from the wall if an intruder is suspected.

E'S LABORATORY

Welcome to E's secret laboratory—a large, ultra-sophisticated work space dedicated to the design, construction, and testing of Super suits! Located below E's elegant home, the laboratory is a place where high-tech gadgetry and high fashion go hand in hand! Designing for supermodels is boring—E likes the challenge of creating fabulous yet functional suits that make Supers look super-stylish!

One thing E insists on when she's crafting a Super suit is NO CAPES! They get snagged on missile tailfins and sucked into jet turbines. They're not just a fashion disaster, they're a *real* disaster waiting to happen!

Tried and tested

After creating Bob's new suit, E decides to design one for each member of the Parr family. Helen's suit is made of an ultra-flexible fabric that can stretch as far as she can. It's virtually indestructible, as E's tests prove!

Helen wasn't expecting such a startling demonstration, but E makes sure all the family's suits are thoroughly tested!

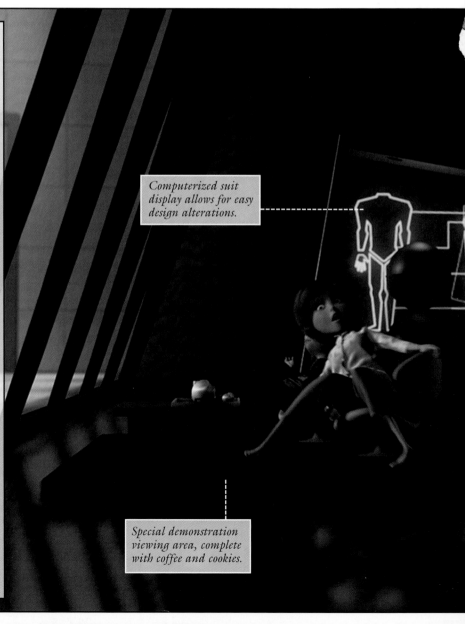

Computerized suit display allows for easy design alterations.

Special demonstration viewing area, complete with coffee and cookies.

Security system

At E's place, the security doesn't stop once you get past the laser beams, electric fence, and Rolf the security guard. To enter her top-secret lab, E must first tap in a 15-digit security code and have her palm-print, retina, and voice pattern analyzed by a computer. Motion sensors can detect if she is alone. Any unauthorized visitors must be cleared by E, or else a huge gun drops down from the ceiling to see them off.

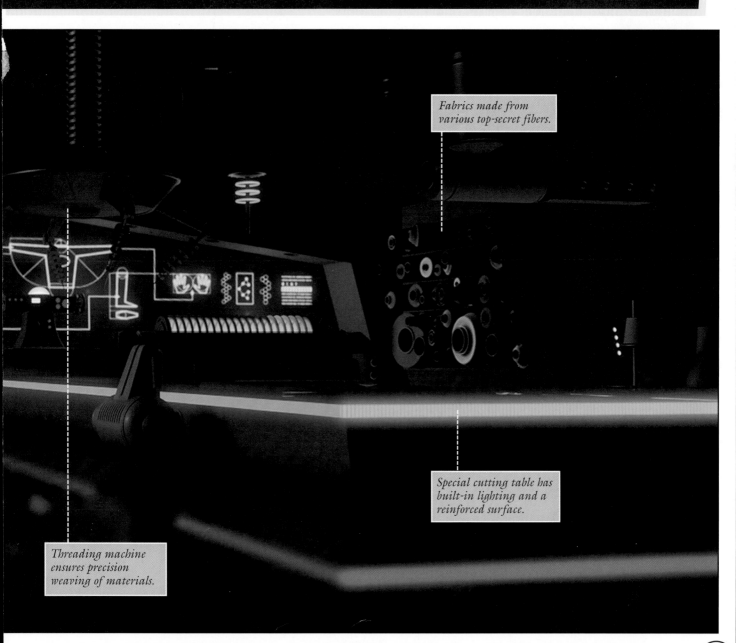

Fabrics made from various top-secret fibers.

Special cutting table has built-in lighting and a reinforced surface.

Threading machine ensures precision weaving of materials.

FALLEN HEROES

In the good old days, there were many different Supers, but after a series of unfortunate lawsuits, their careers ended almost overnight. Forced to blend in with ordinary people, the Supers became civilians, quietly trying to make the world a better place in little ways. But then, years later, the sinister Syndrome appeared with a new use for these has-been heroes....
He tested his secret Omnidroid on them—with devastating results!

Gazerbeam

Tricked into fighting the Omnidroid, Gazerbeam lost his life... but not before he carved the word "KRONOS" on a wall with his laser vision. This last heroic act provides Mr. Incredible with the password to Syndrome's computer and helps him put a stop to the evil genius' secret plans.

MACROBURST

PHYLANGE

APOGEE

BLAZESTONE

GAMMA JACK

DOWNBURST

PSYCWAVE

UNIVERSAL MAN

STORMICIDE

Super weapon

Thanks to Gazerbeam, Mr. Incredible easily gains access to Syndrome's computer. He is stunned when dozens of his friends appear on the screen as victims of Syndrome's Omnidroid. Even Mr. Incredible is marked as terminated.

Cape catastrophes

A cape might seem like an accessory no Super could do without, but in reality, they are a real safety hazard. When you look at the number of Supers who have had cape-related mishaps, it's no wonder E has vowed never to make a cape again....

Mr. Incredible thought Dynaguy had a great look with the boots and the cape, but Dynaguy was all but dynamic when his cape was snagged during takeoff.

Splashdown was another great Super whose cape cost him his life! As he was bravely saving an ocean liner from a freak storm, he was sucked into a vortex.

The story of the dazzling Stratogale is sad but typical. While saving a jet plane with engine trouble, her cape got caught in one of the turbines—and dragged her in after it!

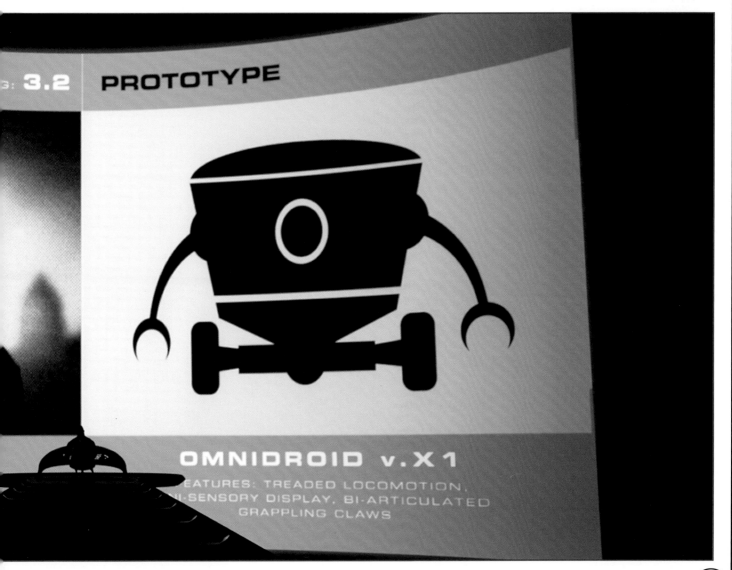

3.2 PROTOTYPE

OMNIDROID v.X1

FEATURES: TREADED LOCOMOTION, MULTI-SENSORY DISPLAY, BI-ARTICULATED GRAPPLING CLAWS

SYNDROME

Syndrome's diabolical hairstyle is a direct result of the power coming from his evil mind.

As a child, Buddy was Mr. Incredible's biggest fan. He made himself a costume and named himself Incrediboy with dreams of being his hero's trusty sidekick… but Mr. Incredible turned him down. Buddy never recovered from being rejected by his idol. He decided that if he couldn't work *with* his idol, he would work *against* him! The hopeless Incrediboy was no more, and in his place stood the fearsome Syndrome!

FEAR IS A GROWTH INDUSTRY.

From an early age, Syndrome was obsessed with Supers. The way he saw it, Supers wore cool outfits and got to beat people up—and the world adored them for it! He vowed that he too would be Super one day. The only trouble was that Buddy didn't have any natural Super powers! That's when his genius for inventing came in extremely handy....

Revenge

When Syndrome captures Mr. Incredible, it is the moment he has spent fifteen years waiting for. But he almost blows it by making a classic villain mistake. He's so pleased with himself, he starts monologuing and allows his attention to wander away from his prisoner.

Evil inventor

Syndrome grew rich by inventing weapons and selling them to the highest bidder. Now, he puts his inventive genius to an even more dreadful use. He plans to unleash his ultimate weapon—the Omnidroid—on the world simply so he can defeat it himself and be loved by the public, just like a Super!

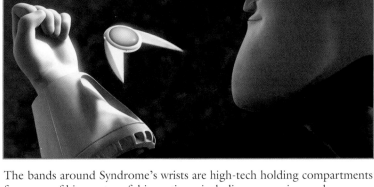

The bands around Syndrome's wrists are high-tech holding compartments for many of his most useful inventions, including a scanning probe, a lollipop bomb, and the remote for his Omnidroid.

Wristband made of polygenic augmenium metal alloy for its durability.

Remote control panel for Omnidroid.

Multifunctional button acts as control key pad and Omnidroid remote control.

INVENTIONS

• The Omnidroid, an intelligent robot that learns how to defeat its opponents.

• The immobi-ray, a deadly weapon that can suspend victims in midair.

• Vector thrust-controlled rocket boots, footwear that enables him to fly.

At the touch of a button in Syndrome's glove, the immobi-ray produces an energy beam so powerful that it paralyzes anyone who's caught in it. The immobi-ray is so effective that even a Super like Mr. Incredible can be suspended in midair with no chance of escape!

MIRAGE

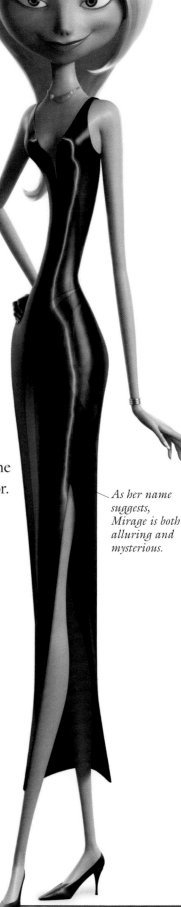

Immaculate platinum-blonde hair.

Every evil villain needs a trusty minion, and they don't come any better than the mysterious Mirage. She's key to the smooth running of all Syndrome's plans. She not only locates retired Supers for him, she tricks them into fighting the deadly Omnidroid! But Mirage is not as ruthless as her employer. She comes to admire Mr. Incredible and his family and finally realizes that her loyalty is wasted on Syndrome.

The target

Mirage follows Frozone, until she realizes that the man with him is Mr. Incredible. She soon switches targets. He is the Super that Syndrome has been looking for.

As her name suggests, Mirage is both alluring and mysterious.

Confident and daring, Mirage finds it easy to infiltrate Insuricare and leave a special package in Bob's briefcase. No one—not even eagle-eyed Gilbert Huph—notices her slipping in and out of the office!

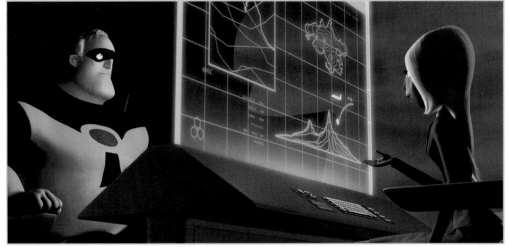

Classified

When Mirage first contacts Mr. Incredible, she tells him that she represents a top-secret division of the government that designs and tests experimental technology. When Mr. Incredible accepts the job, he doesn't know that he will be the subject of a very deadly experiment himself!

Mr. Incredible wonders who Mirage's employer really is, but she's far too discreet to give away any clues to his true identity.

Power-hungry

While dining with Bob, Mirage reveals a key part of her personality—she's attracted to power, just like her employer. It's a weakness they share. But don't think of it as unstable. Mirage prefers to think of it as misunderstood.

Change of heart

Unlike Syndrome, Mirage has a conscience. She is saddened when she sees how devastated Bob is when he thinks his family has been killed. She realizes that Syndrome puts no value on life. When Syndrome gambles with her life in a face-off with Mr. Incredible, Mirage knows it's time to switch sides!

THE OMNIDROID

The Omnidroid is Syndrome's secret battle robot. It's taken the evil genius years to perfect the mean machine, but at last it's ready to be unleashed. The robot is to play a starring role in Syndrome's quest to become a Super. Syndrome plans to release the Omnidroid in the city of Metroville to cause disruption and chaos, just so that *he* can make a dramatic entrance and save the day. Fortunately, things don't quite go to plan!

The Omnidroid would appear to be every villain's dream weapon... but what happens if the machine becomes so smart it decides to give orders, not take them?

PLOT ARC   TARGET LOCK

42.000   29.000

Mighty machine

The Omnidroid is a powerful learning robot. Its artificial intelligence enables it to solve any problem it is confronted with. In fact, every moment it spends fighting its enemies increases its knowledge of how to beat them.

Syndrome spends many years perfecting an Omnidroid worthy of fighting Mr. Incredible. He's gone through seven prototype robots, testing them on unsuspecting Supers. He designs each version to be more deadly than the last, until the Omnidroid is finally ready for Mr. Incredible.

Interlocking armored plates ensure that the legs are well protected yet flexible.

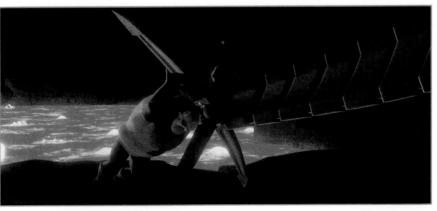

First time lucky?

When he first faces the Omnidroid, Mr. Incredible believes it to be a secret government prototype robot that's on the rampage. His mission is to stop the robot without completely destroying it. Though overweight and out of shape, he eventually manages to defeat it.

Using its lens eye, the robot can track its enemy. It also has various forms of enhanced vision.

Programmed to win

When Mr. Incredible trashes Omnidroid version 8, Syndrome makes some major modifications to the next prototype. With a glaring orange eye, Omnidroid version 9 easily defeats the hero, but Syndrome isn't finished. Before he unleashes his robot on Metroville, he builds version 10—almost ten times the size of version 9, with a faster computer brain.

The Omnidroid is built of incredibly strong, top-secret metal alloys, so it's virtually indestructible.

The simplicity of the ball-like design means that the Omnidroid is an extremely strong structure. Its shape also allows it to travel by rolling.

Splayed foot-claws allow the Omnidroid to grip any surface— even to climb up walls. Built-in thrusters allow for limited flight capability.

Each enormous claw can be used to grasp and crush enemies. The claw can also transform into a deadly spear, drill, or saw blade.

NOMANISAN

From the air, the island of Nomanisan looks like an untamed paradise. It boasts exotic jungles, tumbling waterfalls, tropical lagoons, and even a volcano! When Bob is first taken there in Mirage's manta jet, he believes the island is used for testing high-tech robots, but he soon discovers that there's a far more sinister side to the island....

Hidden deep below the water's surface is the entrance to the secret base. To reach the entrance, the manta jet plunges into the sea and travels to an underwater docking bay.

- - - - - - →

The manta jet's flight path to Syndrome's secret base.

This active volcano is the perfect disguise for Syndrome's base. The molten lava and foul fumes are sure to deter even the nosiest visitor.

This high-speed aircraft is called the "manta jet" because of its similarity to a manta ray fish. The fact that it looks like a sea creature is a clue to one of its most impressive functions—it can transform from a jet to a submersible in seconds!

Teamwork

It's while trapped on Nomanisan that the Incredible family find themselves fighting together for the first time. They soon show Syndrome's guards that, together, they're a force to be reckoned with!

Rocket launch tube.

The entire island is patrolled by Syndrome's army of viper and velocipod units.

Volcanic soil is the most fertile on Earth—all of the guards' rations are grown on the island.

SYNDROME'S ISLAND BASE

There's a lot more to picturesque Nomanisan than meets the eye. Should you peek beneath the island waters, you'll find a huge undersea docking bay that is the gateway to Syndrome's secret base! Costing millions of dollars to build, and fully equipped with super-advanced technology, this secret base is one of the most breathtaking evil lairs in the world!

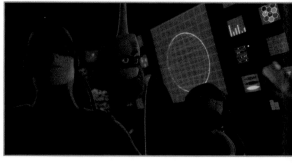

It takes plenty of high-tech gadgets and lots of guards to run Syndrome's secret base. So when Elastigirl enters the control room to find out Bob's location, she must be smart. Luckily, the guards in the control room are so busy checking their screens and read-outs, they don't notice her hanging around!

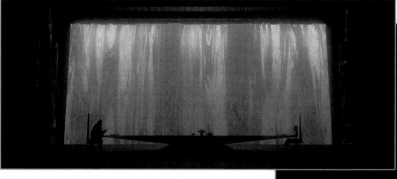

The dining hall overlooks an amazing wall of flowing volcanic lava. But looks are deceptive on this island. The lava wall parts to reveal a secret passageway!

The secret base contains a number of luxury guest suites. Each suite has spectacular ocean views and all the amenities for a comfortable stay!

Suspension arcs

When Mr. Incredible is captured by Syndrome, he's imprisoned in a high-tech jail cell, designed to hold even the strongest Super. A massive electrified holding device dominates the cell. While Mr. Incredible hangs helplessly in its suspension beams, Syndrome sends sparks of painful energy into his body!

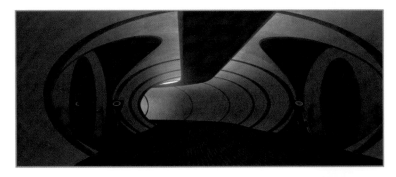

Confusing corridors

Under the surface of Nomanisan, there is a maze of metal corridors that stretches over several miles. Every part of the base can be accessed via this network of tunnels. There are advanced security measures to thwart intruders, and access to the rooms can only be gained with special keycards.

Monopod express

A futuristic monorail network stretches around the island. The transports, called monopods, zoom around the island on elevated tracks. There is also a track system inside the base for speedy travel between areas.

ISLAND SECURITY FORCE

No evil villain with nefarious plans would be properly set up without a force of henchmen to follow their every order. Syndrome's guards are a highly trained, crack combat unit ready to counter any possible threat. The thuggish brutes are armed and extremely dangerous. Anyone setting foot on the island of Nomanisan does so at their own risk....

Tight security

The complex patterns of the henchmen's security rotations keep every bit of Nomanisan well guarded. Only the stealthy Elastigirl is able to penetrate the island's security network.

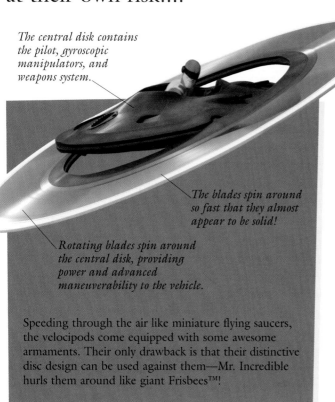

The central disk contains the pilot, gyroscopic manipulators, and weapons system.

The blades spin around so fast that they almost appear to be solid!

Rotating blades spin around the central disk, providing power and advanced maneuverability to the vehicle.

Speeding through the air like miniature flying saucers, the velocipods come equipped with some awesome armaments. Their only drawback is that their distinctive disc design can be used against them—Mr. Incredible hurls them around like giant Frisbees™!

Velocipods

Syndrome's guards have seriously sleek forms of transport. They don't depend on the island's high-tech monorail system to get around—they have the gravity-defying velocipods! These swift, highly maneuverable vehicles are perfect for pursuing irritating intruders through the jungle.

Bird of paradise?

You'd be forgiven for thinking this beautiful, brightly colored bird is native to the tropical island of Nomanisan. But get too close and you'll discover that it's a cleverly disguised security device! Instead of a birdcall, this creature sounds a deafening alarm!

The guards' gray uniforms ensure that they blend in with the metallic decor of the secret base.

Liftoff!

Syndrome's guards watch from base headquarters as the Omnidroid is launched, bound for the city of Metroville. Once Syndrome has left, the henchmen celebrate with a champagne toast—that is, until Mr. Incredible finds them!

Guards receive their orders through a concealed earpiece located on the helmet.

Regulation gray uniform is a bland but functional basic.

Armored, bulletproof vest.

Syndrome's guards have encountered many Supers that have been brought to the island, but they've never had to battle Super kids before! Dash runs rings around them, while Violet disappears on them! It's enough to drive a security guard crazy!

LONDON, NEW YORK, MUNICH,
MELBOURNE, AND DELHI

ART EDITOR Dan Bunyan
PROJECT EDITOR Lindsay Fernandes
ART DIRECTOR Mark Richards
PUBLISHING MANAGER Cynthia O'Neill Collins
CATEGORY PUBLISHER Alex Kirkham
PRODUCTION Nicola Torode
DTP DESIGNER Dean Scholey

First American Edition, 2004
Published in the United States by
DK Publishing, Inc., 375 Hudson Street, New York, New York 10014

04 05 06 07 08 10 9 8 7 6 5 4 3 2 1

A Cataloging-in-Publication record for this book is available from the Library of Congress.

ISBN 0-7566-0551-2

Reproduced by Media Development and Printing Ltd., U.K.
Printed and bound in the United States by R. R. Donnelley & Sons, U.S.A.

Acknowledgments

Dorling Kindersley would like to thank:
Krista Swager, Mark Andrews, Leeann Alameda, Kathleen Chanover, Ed Chen, Jeff Raymond,
Holly Lloyd, Bert Berry, and Kate Ranson-Walsh at Pixar Animation Studios;
Lisa Gerstel, Esther Kim, Hunter Heller, Graham Barnard, and Tim Lewis at Disney Publishing.

Discover more at
www.dk.com